Contents

You can find words shown in bold, **like this,** in the Glossary.

What is cotton?

Cotton is a **natural** material. It comes from cotton plants. We normally see cotton when it has been made into clothes. But on the plant it looks like fluffy white hair.

We use cotton to make cotton **fabrics**. The fabrics are made into clothes, sheets and cloths. All the things here are made from cotton.

Cotton fibres

A **fibre** is a long, thin thread. For example, a single hair from your head is a fibre. Cotton fibres grow from the seeds of cotton plants.

The shortest cotton fibres are about 2 centimetres long. The longest ones are about 6 centimetres long. This is what cotton fibres look like through a **microscope**.

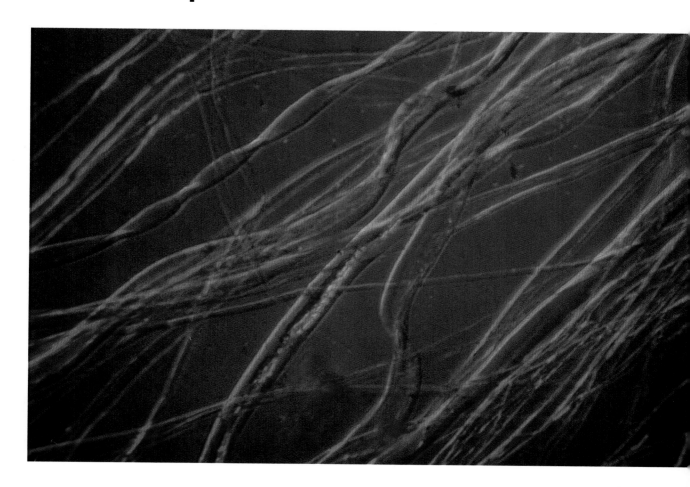

Properties of cotton fibres

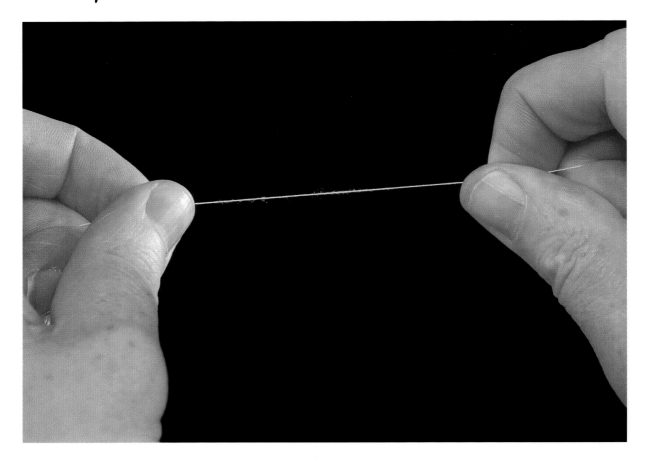

Cotton **fibres** are thinner than the hairs on your head. But they are still quite strong. They are good for making tough thread called **yarn**. Cotton fibres are white or light grey.

Water soaks into cotton fibres easily. Even when the fibres are wet, they are still strong. It is easy to change the colour of cotton fibres with **chemicals** called **dyes**.

Growing cotton

Cotton plants only grow in places where the weather is warm and sunny all year round. The **fibres** grow after the flowers have blossomed and died.

Collecting the fibres from the cotton
plants is called harvesting. Harvesting
machines move over the plants. They
pull the fibres off the plants and
collect them up.

Processing cotton

The cotton from the harvesting machines is taken to a factory to be **processed**. This cotton has been dried, and twigs and dirt have been taken out.

When cotton **fibres** are harvested
they are still attached to cotton seeds.
A machine called a cotton gin
separates the fibres and seeds. The
fibres are gathered into fluffy bundles.

Spinning yarn

Most cotton is made into cotton **yarn**.
The cotton arrives at the spinning
factory in big **bales**. It is unpacked and
the **fibres** are combed to sort them out.

The fibres are gathered into a long,
thin bunch. Then the bunch is twisted
to make the fibres grip each other
tightly. This is called **spinning** the yarn.

Weaving and Knitting

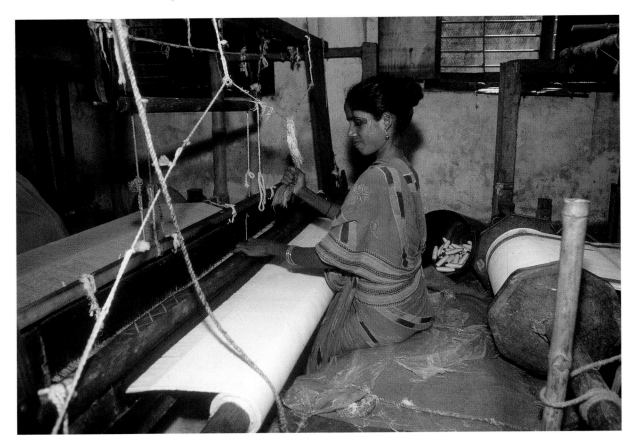

Cotton **yarn** is made into cotton **fabric** by **weaving** or **knitting**. Weaving is done by a machine called a loom. A loom makes fabric by threading pieces of yarn over and under each other.

A knitting machine makes cotton fabric by joining tiny loops of yarn. This picture shows a blue woven fabric and a white knitted fabric.

Colour and pattern

Coloured cotton **fabric** can be made by using **yarn** that has already been **dyed**. Sometimes the fabric is dyed after it has been woven or **knitted**.

Fabrics with patterns are made by
weaving different coloured yarns
together. Coloured patterns can also
be printed on to plain cotton fabric.
This pattern is being printed by hand.

Cotton clothes

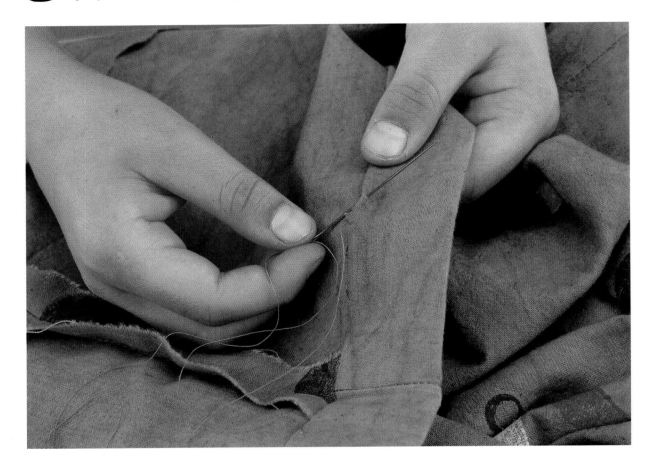

We make cotton clothes by cutting
out pieces of cotton **fabric**. The pieces
are sewn together with cotton **yarn**.
Shirts, T-shirts, trousers and dresses
can all be made from cotton fabrics.

Cotton is a good material for making summer clothes. Cotton fabric can be light in weight and cool to wear. But it can also be made into tough clothes, such as denim jeans.

Cotton around us

We also use cotton **fabrics** to make sheets and pillow cases, curtains and tablecloths. People use cotton **yarn** to sew pictures. This is called embroidery.

22

Towels are made of cotton. They are good for drying your wet body or wet dishes. The cotton **fibres** soak up water well.

Cotton wool and paper

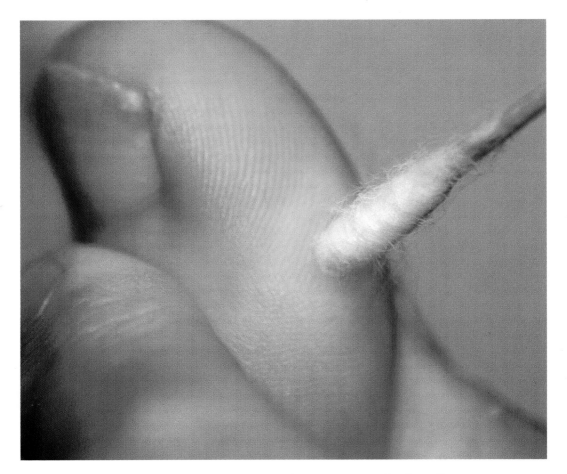

Not all cotton is made into **fabric**.
Some cotton is made into cotton
wool and cotton buds. They are
used for first aid and for putting
on make-up.

Paper is made from wood **fibres** mixed with water and glue. Cotton fibres can be mixed with the wood fibres to make strong, fine paper.

More uses for cotton

Only the **fibres** from cotton plants are used for making **yarn** and **fabrics**. The inside parts of cotton seeds are crushed to make cotton oil. The **husks** are given to cattle to eat.

Some cotton fibres are too short for making yarn. They are gathered together to make soft **padding** for furniture and car seats.

Fact file

▶ Cotton is a **natural** material. It grows on cotton plants.

▶ Cotton **fibres** are thin but strong.

▶ Cotton is made stronger by **spinning** it to make **yarn**.

▶ Cotton soaks up water well.

▶ Natural cotton is white or grey when it grows.

▶ Cotton can be coloured with **dyes**.

▶ Cotton burns when it is heated.

▶ Cotton does not let **electricity** flow through it.

▶ Cotton is not attracted by magnets.

Would you believe it?

We use lots of cotton to make clothes. If all the cotton grown in different countries was put in a heap, the heap would weigh 20 million tonnes!

Glossary

bale huge bundle made of many fibres or pieces of fabric pressed together

chemicals special materials that are used in factories and homes to do many jobs, including cleaning

dye something that changes the colour of fibres and fabrics

electricity form of energy. We use electricity to make electric machines work.

fabric woven or knitted material, such as cloth

fibre thin thread of a material

husk tough case on the outside of a seed

knitting making fabric by joining tiny loops of yarn

microscope something that makes things look much bigger than they really are. It is used to look at tiny things.

natural comes from plants, animals or the rocks in the Earth

padding soft material that is put inside chairs to make them soft to sit on. It is put in jackets to make them warm.

process to prepare something for use. Cotton has to be cleaned and dried before it can be used to make yarn.

spinning making long pieces of yarn by twisting fibres together

weaving making fabric by threading yarns over and under each other

yarn long string of material made by twisting fibres together

More books to read

Images: Materials and Their Properties
Big Book Compilation
Heinemann Library, 1999

My World of Science
Angela Royston
Heinemann Library, 2001

New Star Science: Materials and Their Uses
Ginn, 2001

Science Files: Textiles
Steve Parker
Heinemann Library, 2001

Why T-shirts are Cotton
Mary Schoeser
Longmann, 2001

Index